What makes hot air balloons fly?

DK Direct Limited
Managing Art Editor Eljay Crompton
Senior Editor Rosemary McCormick
Writer Alexandra Parsons
Illustrators The Alvin White Studios and Richard Manning
Designers Wayne Blades, Veneta Bullen, Richard Clemson,
Sarah Goodwin, Diane Klein, Sonia Whillock

Photo image on page 6 courtesy of the Kobal Collection © RKO Studio

Contents

How did people get around before cars, bikes, and trains?

If they couldn't afford to buy a horse, they walked or else they stayed home. People just didn't travel around the way they do now. Some people lived all their lives within walking distance of one place, and so did their children, and their children's children.

Carry me, please
Some people who didn't like to walk were carried. The rickshaw is a two-wheeled chair which is either pulled or pushed. It was first used in Japan about 150 years ago.

Going my way

The sedan chair was a popular way to get around crowded streets long ago. It was a closed chair carried on poles by either two or four people.

Put on your walking shoes

 Humans start to learn to walk when they are about one year old.

 A comfortable walking speed is about three miles an hour.

 The first person to walk around the world was an American named David Kunst. It took him over four years. (He crossed oceans by ship or plane.)

How far can you go in a horse and cart?

Only as far as the horse wants to go! Horses need rest, water, and food, just as we do. Before cars and trains were invented, horses pulled coaches along dirt roads at about eight miles an hour. Some coaches were called stagecoaches because the journey was made in stages. The drivers stopped to pick up a team of fresh horses every 15 miles or so, at inns along the way.

Getting around
Some people used public stagecoaches to get around, and some people had their own private carriages like this one called a surrey.

What a way to travel!

 Wells, Fargo & Company ran the first express coach service between the east and west of America. One hundred and twenty years ago it took 25 bumpy, dusty days to travel from Missouri to California.

 Early settlers making the long trek west with no fresh horses took six months to make the same journey.

What is the difference between a boat and a ship?

Ships are bigger than boats! A ship can carry a boat, a boat can carry smaller boats, but a boat CAN'T carry a ship. A big cruise ship, for instance, will carry lots of lifeboats – just in case!

Zooming along
Speed boats are small, fast boats that zoom through the water. They are used for fun and for racing.

Sick ship
Where does a sick
ship go?
To the dock.

Shipping and boating facts

☞ One of the largest cruise ships in the world is the Norway. It has room for 2,400 passengers. And then there are hundreds of crew who have to look after them!

☞ Some cargo ships are so big that the crew use bikes to get around the deck.

What makes hot air balloons fly?

The hot air! Hot air, you see, is lighter than cool or warm air. So if hot air can be trapped inside a balloon, the balloon will be lighter than the air that surrounds it, and up it will go!

Heat it up!

This is how the air inside the balloon gets hot. The pilot in the basket turns up the heat on a giant gas burner. The air is kept hot by occasional blasts of heat from the burner.

Cool it down!

When it's time to come down to earth, the pilot turns off the heat so the air inside the balloon cools down. It lands with a gentle bump.

Flying farmyard

☞ The first living creatures to fly were a sheep, a duck and a rooster. They were sent up by the inventors of the hot air balloon to check that the balloon was safe. Sounds like a job for Old MacDonald!

Why do trains need tracks?

Because train wheels run better on fixed tracks, and they don't slip and slide or get stuck in the mud when carrying heavy loads. Some of the first steam trains puffed carefully along wooden rails at about 20 mph. Today, train tracks are made of steel, and some trains can zip along ten times faster, at about 200 mph.

Clickety clack!

Traveling by train on long journeys can be fun. You can dine in the dining car – and watch the countryside flash by as you munch on lunch. And at nighttime you can snuggle under the blankets in a sleeping car.

Tricky track

People have put railway tracks in amazing places. Some lines go through mountains and even under rivers.

Just one

Trains that run on one wide central track are called monorails.

Down the line

Lady: A round trip ticket, please.
Conductor: Where to?
Lady: Back here, of course!

How fast can you go on a bike?

As fast as your legs will pedal! A fit person on a good bike can ride along comfortably at about 15 miles an hour. Bike racing is a different matter. Track racers can fly along at 50 miles an hour! That's almost the speed limit for cars!

Out of my way! This racing bike was designed to be REALLY fast, and very light. You'd get to school really quickly on one of these!

Look, no hands! Unicycles are cycles with just one wheel and no handlebars. They are quite tricky to ride, but some people have managed to cycle across America on unicycles.

Cycle stories

☞ The tallest unicycle ever ridden is almost 102 feet tall!

☞ A team of 32 divers, in California, pedaled almost 117 miles under water on a tricycle. It took them 75 hours and 20 minutes.

Why do cars need gasoline?

Because gasoline is the fuel that makes car engines go. Car engines work by burning gasoline. An electric spark lights the fuel and as it burns it creates hot gases. The gases power the engine and this makes the wheels go around.

Drilling for oil
Gasoline for cars is made from oil. Oil is found in many places all over the world. It is often found deep beneath the ocean.

Clank, clank
What happens when a
frog's car breaks down?
He gets toad away.

Gassy facts

 The bad thing about burning fuel is
fumes! Scientists are trying to find
other ways to make engines go. So
far we've got cars that run on
batteries, cars that run on alcohol
made from sugar cane, and cars
that run on methane gas that
comes from rotting vegetables and
animal droppings.

What is a cable car?

It is a passenger car attached to a cable that is always moving. One of the first cable car systems was built in the hilly city of San Francisco. To move the car, the driver pulls a lever that makes the car grip onto the cable. To stop, the driver pushes the lever to let go of the cable. Simple, isn't it?

Skiing uphill
Ski lifts also work by gripping onto overhead cables. The cables pull skiers up mountains so they can ski back down. Wheeee!

Stick to the rails!
Rollercoasters work in a similar way. Cables pull the cars up the hills, then the cars let go of the cables and down they go!

Van Ness Ave.. California
58
& Market Stre

Cable facts

 Each week, in San Francisco, more than 200,000 people ride the cable cars.

 The longest roller coaster in the world is 1.4 miles. It's called The Big Beast and it's near Cincinnati, Ohio.

Which city first had subways?

London. In 1863 an underground railway was built by digging a big trench, laying the track in it and then building an arched roof over the top. Just like today, people used the subway to get to work quickly without getting stuck in traffic.

Busy, busy
The world's busiest subway is the one in Moscow. More than three and a half billion people use it each year.

Puff, puff
The first subway trains were powered by steam and lit by gaslight. Imagine how smoky and smelly it was down there?

Special subway statistics

 The first American city to have a subway was Boston.

 The subway system with the most stations is the one in New York. It has 469 stations and carries five million passengers a day.

Which is the world's fastest plane?

The fastest passenger plane is the Concorde, which zooms along at 1,450 miles an hour – more than twice the speed of sound. That's fast! Ordinary jet airliners fly at speeds of about 550 mph.

Blink, and you'll miss it!

The fastest military plane is the Lockheed SR-71A, which holds the official airspeed record of 2,193.167 miles an hour. It's so fast that if it began a journey around the world as you were having breakfast, it would be back again at bedtime.

Super speed facts

The speeds that things can move at in our everyday lives can be as slow as a snail or as fast as a supersonic jet. Scientists believe that the speed of light is the fastest possible speed – that's 186,281 miles per second!

How do helicopters fly without wings?

Well, they DO have wings, but they aren't like airplane wings. They look like blades, and a powerful engine whirls them around and around very fast. The helicopter's whizzing blades lift and support the helicopter and drive it through the air. The tail blades stop the helicopter from spinning around.

Happy landings! The maple tree seed pod drops from the tree and is whirled away on the wind, just like a little flying helicopter.

Staying put!

Helicopters are one of the few flying machines that can stay up in the air without moving forward or backward. They can be used to rescue people from the most awkward places.

Whirly facts

 Helicopters can fly backward, forward, and sideways.

The seeds of some trees, like maples and sycamores, have helicopter-type wings so they can fly far away from the parent tree and find rich soil to grow in.

How do rockets take off?

They get pushed up into the air by a huge, explosive boost of hot gases. The gases push against the rocket and send it soaring upward. The hot gases come from burning very large amounts of fuel.

Whoosh!
Fireworks get pushed up into the sky by setting fire to the gunpowder inside them. Burning gunpowder creates a whoosh of gases!

Pushing backward to go forward

If you blow up a balloon, and let it go without tying the neck, the balloon will be pushed forward by the air streaming out.

Rocket facts

☞ The Chinese invented a kind of rocket about a thousand years ago! They made rocket-powered arrows, powered by gunpowder, to aim at their enemies.

☞ The reason space rockets are so big is because they have to carry so much fuel.

Can you spot the differences between these two pictures? There are six things missing from picture B. Can you find them?

A

B

Answers: steam from train; person on path; helicopter blades; balloon basket; ship's funnel; wheel spokes.